Mr Cadabra
a magician

Huge
a giant

Enorma
a giant, Huge's wife

3

Scene One
Outside Widow Do-Nothing's house

Enter Widow Do-Nothing.

Widow Do-Nothing *(to audience)* Hello, ladies and gentlemen, boys and girls. I want to tell you about my son, Jack. I think he must be the laziest boy in the whole world! Do you know, he even sleeps in his clothes because he's too lazy to get dressed in the morning! Here he comes …

Enter Jack, yawning.

Jack What am I going to have for breakfast, Mother? There's no bread left. And there's no milk … no jam … in fact there's nothing to eat at all.

Widow Do-Nothing Oh dear! Has it got as bad as that? No money and now – no food. There's nothing else for it – I'm going to have to sell you!

Jack Sell me? You can't sell your own son!

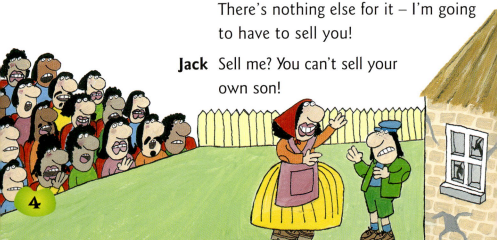

4

Jack and the Beanstalk

A pantomime retold by Marilyn Finlay

Illustrations by Carla Daly

Cast

Widow Do-Nothing No, I can't. (*Pause for a laugh*) No one would buy you! Well, if it's not you, it will have to be Daisy. At least she's worth something.

Enter Daisy.

Daisy Did someone mention my name?

Jack Mother says we've got to sell you.

Daisy (*to audience*) Boys and girls! What do you think of a woman who would turn a poor cow out of the only home she's ever known?

Audience Boo! Hiss!

Jack (*yawning*) It's all right, Daisy. I'm too tired to walk all the way to market with you anyway.

Widow Do-Nothing You lazy boy, Jack!

Suddenly, in a puff of smoke, Mr Cadabra appears.

Mr Cadabra Sorry to startle you, ladies and gents. Cadabra's the name. Magic's my game! I may be able to help you.

5

*Daisy trots round and stands behind
Mr Cadabra.*

Mr Cadabra Now, where's
this cow?

Audience She's behind you!

Mr Cadabra Behind me? Oh,
you mean here.

*Daisy trots round behind Mr Cadabra as he turns
to face the other way.*

Mr Cadabra Where's she gone now?

Audience She's behind you!

Mr Cadabra turns back quickly, and comes face to face with Daisy.

Daisy & Mr Cadabra Boo!

Widow Do-Nothing You've caught us at a bad moment,
Mr Magic Wizard Cadabra or
whatever your name is. We've no
food and no money.

Mr Cadabra Hurray, hurrah, let the bells chime.
I've come to your rescue in the nick
of time!

Daisy Is he mad? What's he talking about?

Jack Excuse me, Mr Cadabra, but is your
first name Abra?

Mr Cadabra Oh, blow! Why does everybody always
guess it? You can all call me Abe.

Widow Do-Nothing And how are you going to rescue us, Abe? *(laughs behind hand)* Conjure up some money with a magic spell?

Mr Cadabra Well I would, but my spells usually go wrong. Can't think why. But … your problems are solved.
I'll tell you how.
I'm going to buy your beautiful cow!

Jack We need a lot of money for her.

Daisy *(boasting)* I'm a beautiful, intelligent cow who can talk.

Mr Cadabra *(to Daisy)* I know. *(To Widow Do-Nothing)* And that's why I'm prepared to make you a once in a lifetime offer. For your wonderful talking cow, I'm going to give you these superb … beans.

Mr Cadabra gives Widow Do-Nothing a handful of beans.

Widow Do-Nothing looks at them. She is not impressed.

Widow Do-Nothing Beans? What use are they?

Mr Cadabra They're magic beans. Amazing things will happen if you plant them.

7

Jack That sounds like hard work.

Daisy I think you should take the beans. I'd like to go with Mr Cadabra. He's got lovely long eyelashes. He reminds me of my mother.

Mr Cadabra *(to Daisy)* Do call me Abe, my dear. *(To Widow Do-Nothing)* Right, that's settled. I'll take the cow, you know what that means, and leave you to sow your magic beans!

Daisy Let's hit the road, Abe!

Mr Cadabra Certainly, my dear. By the way, do you know what game cows like to play at parties?

Daisy No. What game do cows like to play at parties?

Mr Cadabra Moo-sical chairs! Get it, moo ... sical.

Daisy Moo ... sical chairs! Oh, that's good, very good.

Mr Cadabra and Daisy exit, laughing.

8

Widow Do-Nothing *(to audience)* Well that's just wonderful. I've got no money, no food, and now, I've got no cow. All I've got is a useless son. *(To Jack)* You'd better get on and sow these beans. I don't suppose anything will happen, but you never know …

Widow Do-Nothing gives Jack the beans and exits.

Jack *(to audience)* I'm fed up. Mother's always saying how lazy I am, but she's no better. You ought to see her bedroom. She never cleans it, and it smells so bad that even the cockroaches won't go in there! I can't be bothered to sow these beans. I'll just throw them away and go to bed. I've been up for nearly two hours already!

Jack throws the beans on the ground and then exits, yawning.

Scene Two

The next morning, outside Widow Do-Nothing's house.
A large beanstalk has appeared. It reaches up into the sky.

Enter Widow Do-Nothing.

Widow Do-Nothing *(singing)* Oh, what a beautiful morning! Oh, what a beautiful day! I've got a … Ooh, what on Earth is that?

Enter Jack, yawning.

Jack Can't you sing more quietly? That's funny. That tree wasn't there yesterday. At least, I didn't notice it.

Widow Do-Nothing You stupid boy! It's grown from the beans that wizard gave us. Jack, fan me with one of the leaves, I feel faint!

Jack Get a leaf and fan yourself!

Widow Do-Nothing Do I have to do everything around here?

Jack *(suddenly interested)* What a huge stalk! I'm going to climb up it and see where it leads.

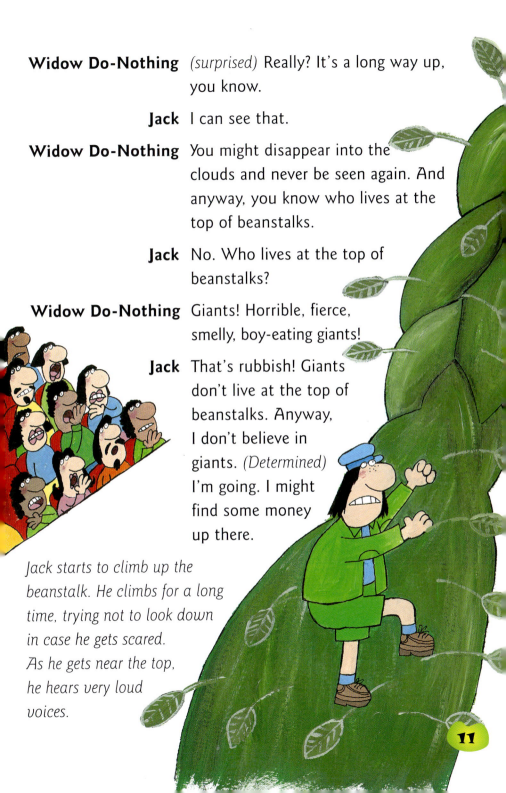

Widow Do-Nothing *(surprised)* Really? It's a long way up, you know.

Jack I can see that.

Widow Do-Nothing You might disappear into the clouds and never be seen again. And anyway, you know who lives at the top of beanstalks.

Jack No. Who lives at the top of beanstalks?

Widow Do-Nothing Giants! Horrible, fierce, smelly, boy-eating giants!

Jack That's rubbish! Giants don't live at the top of beanstalks. Anyway, I don't believe in giants. *(Determined)* I'm going. I might find some money up there.

Jack starts to climb up the beanstalk. He climbs for a long time, trying not to look down in case he gets scared. As he gets near the top, he hears very loud voices.

11

Scene Three

The giants' house, at the top of the beanstalk

Huge and Enorma are sitting at the kitchen table, chatting.

Enorma I'm not making any more breakfast. Three sheep and a cow are enough for anyone. If I give you any more, you won't eat your lunch.

Huge I always eat my lunch. You know that. I'm always hungry. And do you know, I think I can smell something delicious!

Enorma I don't know what it can be. I'm not cooking anything.

Huge Fee, fi, fo, foy, I smell the blood of a juicy boy!

Enorma Will you stop all that fee, fi, fo, foy stuff! You know I hate it.

Huge It's what giants do, you silly old thing! You have to do it, or you're not a proper giant.

Enorma Well my mother and father were proper giants, and they didn't go around fee, fi, fo, foy-ing all the time. And I don't do it.

Huge Well I was brought up to believe you had to do it at least once a week. But really, I can smell something.

Jack comes in; he is very scared.

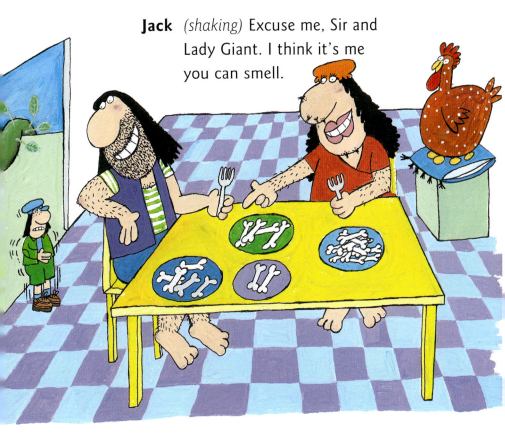

Jack *(shaking)* Excuse me, Sir and Lady Giant. I think it's me you can smell.

Huge *(to Enorma)* What do I do now? I won't have to eat him, will I?

Jack *(scared)* I hope you won't.

Enorma I've never seen one of those before. He's rather sweet.

Jack *(shyly)* My mother and I haven't got any money and we wondered if you had any to spare.

13

Enorma *(to Jack)* We don't really bother with money. *(To Huge)* Look at his tiny little fingers!

Huge *(pointing to Clucky)* We've got Clucky, the hen. She lays eggs made of gold, so we use those instead. I still think I really ought to eat you.

Jack Please don't. My mother would be so upset if ...

Suddenly, there is a great creaking sound and the beanstalk shakes from side to side. Widow Do-Nothing steps off it. She is very out of breath.

Jack That **is** my mother! *(To Widow Do-Nothing)* How did you get up here?

Widow Do-Nothing *(trying to get her breath back)* Same way as you – I climbed. And I'm too old for climbing. But I couldn't let my baby boy go all by himself, could I?

Huge He might get eaten.

Widow Do-Nothing You wouldn't do that, would you? Not a big, handsome man like you. I like a man to be tall.

Enorma *(crossly)* **Of course he's tall – he's a giant. And I'm his wife.**

Widow Do-Nothing *(curtseying)* Delighted to meet you. Now I know such good-looking, kind, intelligent people wouldn't bother with such a little bit of nothing as my son, Jack.

Jack Thanks very much!

Widow Do-Nothing We'll be off now. It has been charming to meet you, and I do hope you'll drop in for tea one day.

Widow Do-Nothing starts to climb down the beanstalk. Jack grabs Clucky and follows closely behind.

Enorma Hey! Where do you think you're going?

Huge And you've got Clucky. *(To Enorma)* **Quick, after them!**

Huge and Enorma start to climb down the beanstalk. They are very slow. Jack and Widow Do-Nothing are a long way ahead.

Scene Four

Outside Widow Do-Nothing's house

Enter Daisy and Mr Cadabra.

Daisy　I think they're both out. I mooed a few times but there was no reply.

Mr Cadabra　Shall I do some magic while we wait?

Daisy　No, your spells never work. I'm fed up. I thought they'd be here.

Mr Cadabra　When you feel sad, I put on my cloak. I wave my wand, and tell you a joke … Knock, knock.

Daisy　Who's there?

Mr Cadabra　Amos.

Daisy　Amos who?

Mr Cadabra　*(laughing)* A mosquito bit me!

Daisy　Very funny. Where are they?

Mr Cadabra　I'll tell you another one. Knock, knock …

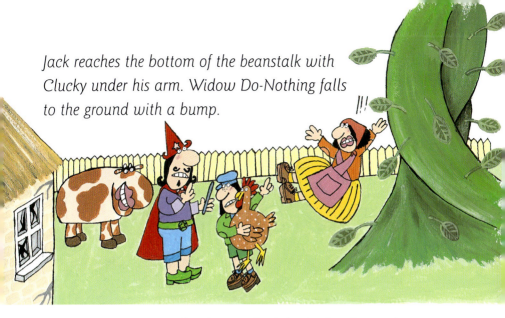

Jack reaches the bottom of the beanstalk with Clucky under his arm. Widow Do-Nothing falls to the ground with a bump.

Jack *(to Mr Cadabra)* Thank goodness you're here. A giant is going to eat me!

Widow Do-Nothing I've never been so flustered in all my life! I could tell Mr Giant liked me. It was only his horrid wife who wanted to chase us.

Jack Quick! There's no time to lose!

Mr Cadabra Right …
My magic's strong so have no fear –
all giants now will disappear!

Daisy That didn't work. Look, the beanstalk is shaking! They'll be here soon.

Widow Do-Nothing Oh dear, I think I'm going to faint. Somebody do something!

Mr Cadabra I could try another spell …

All No!

Daisy If I felt really hungry, I could probably chew through that stalk, and then the giants would fall down. Trouble is, I've just had lunch.

Jack Please try, Daisy. We'll think of delicious food that might make you hungry.

Daisy All right, I'll try.

Daisy starts chewing at the beanstalk.

Widow Do-Nothing Soft green grass!

Mr Cadabra Chocolate cake!

Jack Strawberries and cream!

Daisy It's no good. I can't do it. It's too thick.

Widow Do-Nothing *(to audience)* Boys and girls – will you help us? Make Daisy feel hungry by shouting out all the nicest food you can think of.

Audience Ice cream! Jelly! Chocolate éclairs.

Daisy I'm nearly there. Keep shouting.

The audience calls out more food, until there is a great creak.
Daisy bites through the beanstalk, and it comes tumbling to the
ground. Huge and Enorma tumble with it.

Huge *(rubbing head)* Ow! My head!
I bumped it on the ground.

Enorma I feel dizzy, we came down
so suddenly.

Mr Cadabra Look for me low, look for me high.
I'll fight you giants until you die!

Huge That's not a very nice thing to say.

Jack *(scared)* Please don't eat me! I'm sorry
I took your hen.

Enorma Eat you? Of course he won't eat you.
He's never eaten anybody.

Widow Do-Nothing I knew such a charming, attractive giant would be kind. You wouldn't hurt a teeny, weeny boy, would you?

Enorma You can keep your eyes off my husband. He wouldn't look at you anyhow. He likes them a bit younger.

Widow Do-Nothing I'm only 20.

Daisy Times three!

Widow Do-Nothing glares at Daisy.

Huge I don't want to eat anyone. Look, if you'll let us have milk from Daisy – say once a week – you can keep Clucky the hen. What do you say?

Jack Thank you, Mr Huge. You're very kind. I'm going to tell everyone not to be afraid of giants anymore.

Mr Cadabra I'm sorry about what I said before. To make up for it, let me tell you a joke.

Huge Oh good, I love jokes!

Mr Cadabra Knock, knock …

Huge Who's there?

Mr Cadabra Lucy.

All Lucy who?

Mr Cadabra Loose elastic makes your pants fall down!

Everyone laughs except Widow Do-Nothing.

Widow Do-Nothing Mr Cadabra! What will our new friends think of us?

The others are still laughing. Widow Do-Nothing comes forward.

Widow Do-Nothing *(to audience)* Now our story's at an end, the giants have become our friends. We fill our days with jokes and laughter, and we'll all live happily ever after.

21

READY, STEADY, ACT!

This play is a pantomime, so the audience joins in the fun.

CHOOSING THE PARTS

Choose who will play each part.

- Jack is a lazy boy.
- Widow Do-Nothing is Jack's mother. She is the 'Dame'. The person playing this part (girl or boy) needs to be confident and funny.
- Daisy the talking cow is lovable and sensible.
- Mr Cadabra is a mysterious magician who speaks in rhyme.
- Huge and Enorma, the giant and his wife, need loud booming voices. They could be played by boys.
- Have a few friends in the audience who know what to reply.

SETTING THE SCENE

Pantomime sets are usually like cartoons – bright and colourful. Some jolly music would help set the scene. How will you play Daisy – will you use two people?

Did you know…?
Pantomime dames have been played for laughs by men dressed as women for nearly 200 years.

WHAT YOU WILL NEED

Costumes

Anything colourful and very silly will work in this pantomime.

- Widow Do-Nothing could wear a big dress, a wig if you can get one, and lots of make-up.
- Jack could wear jeans and a bright T-shirt.
- Mr Cadabra will need a cloak and a wizard's hat.
- The giants could do with some padding.
- If Daisy is played by two actors, they will need to be draped in a sheet with large spots. The front could wear horns on a headband.

Props

Make a props list from the text. How will you manage the beanstalk? Mime it? Use a real plant? Make it from string and paper leaves?

Sound effects

A Swanee whistle would work well for going up and down the beanstalk. When it falls, make a clatter with dustbin lids or a clash of cymbals.

Special effects

Signal Mr Cadabra's sudden entrance with a loud bang.

SPEAKING AND MOVING

Speaking

All the dialogue in a pantomime has to be larger than life! When you talk to the audience, make sure that you meet someone's eye and don't forget to smile. Encourage the audience to join in the booing or shouting. You could say things like, 'I can't hear you.'

Moving

Do giants move differently from people? How might they move?

You will need to mime some of the actions in this play – climbing the beanstalk and falling down. This means not actually climbing on anything, so remember to keep safe. Have a go at miming climbing up and getting tired as you go. What will happen if you look down? Practise falling in slow motion with your arms up and slowly bending your knees.

What next?

- Find some music to start and finish the play.
- Astonish your family and friends with a brilliant performance.